How to
IMPROVE
Classroom
DISCIPLINE

An Action Checklist

Printed in Victoria, Canada

National Library of Canada Cataloguing in Publication

Hempel, Mervin, 1944-
    How to improve classroom discipline / Mervin Hempel.
ISBN 1-4120-0850-6
    1. Classroom management. 2. School discipline. I. Title.
LB3013.H45 2004   371.5   C2003-904639-7

TRAFFORD

This book was published on-demand in cooperation with Trafford Publishing.
On-demand publishing is a unique process and service of making a book available for retail sale to the public taking advantage of on-demand manufacturing and Internet marketing. On-demand publishing includes promotions, retail sales, manufacturing, order fulfilment, accounting and collecting royalties on behalf of the author.

Suite 6E, 2333 Government St., Victoria, B.C. V8T 4P4, CANADA
Phone   250-383-6864   Toll-free   1-888-232-4444 (Canada & US)
Fax 250-383-6804   E-mail sales@trafford.com   Web site www.trafford.com
TRAFFORD PUBLISHING IS A DIVISION OF TRAFFORD HOLDINGS LTD.
Trafford Catalogue #03-1218   www.trafford.com/robots/03-1218.html

10   9   8   7   6   5   4   3

To my wife Judith, our son Bradley and our daughter Jennifer

Introduction

One of the top priorities facing schools today is solving discipline problems. This is an obvious fact to those of us involved in education. Schools cannot move forward in an efficient and productive manner without the essential element of good discipline.

Teacher morale has taken a beating because of the effects of classroom discipline problems. Stress, burnout and a change in professions are some of the results of those problems. Student academic performance suffers which has a diminishing effect on human potential.

The primary audience for this book are teachers and school personnel at the elementary and junior high levels. Its purpose is to help teachers encourage appropriate behavior in children in order to improve their performance, in both the academic and behavioral areas. It assumes that if students are behaving appropriately in the classroom and are on task, then they will learn more no matter what educational techniques or methodologies are used.

The suggestions found in this book are a combination of traditional approaches and ideas as fresh as freshly squeezed orange juice. They attempt to help develop an atmosphere in which each individual's rights are respected; and at the same time these ideas encourage the belief that without individuals showing responsibility, there can be no rights.

This book can be used in at least two different ways. First as a reference guide. For example, use it if you are faced with a specific discipline problem as shown by a student who is exhibiting loud disrespectful behavior in class. As we read the various ideas we will be stimulated into thinking of a solution which uniquely fits the immediate problem situation.

Second, trying different approaches can help us refine our teaching styles, adjust to differing student reactions and to discover which techniques work best for us. Better yet, let's hope that "How to Improve Classroom Discipline" prompts you to discover fresh and original ideas!

This book is organized as a collection of one hundred and eleven tried and tested ideas for handling all kinds of everyday classroom problems and for encouraging student self-control. This action checklist allows you to quickly skim through the techniques and decide which ones to use. The ideas are easy to plug into your existing classroom management style.

It is not expected that every reader will approve of and accept all of the suggestions offered here. What works for one teacher may not work for another. However, if the reader gleans just two or three ideas that will lead toward better classroom management, then writing the book has been well worth the effort.

Contents

1

GENERAL
INTERVENTIONS

General Interventions

Starting the Year

After completing orientation, start the year's studies in earnest. Simultaneously, and positively, teach behavioral expectations. This should last for a few weeks or more depending on the class.

Set standards for students especially those covering chatter and safety. Students enjoy making suggestions for classroom rules and expectations. Actively teach the rules. Any effective method will do. Don't just hang a list on the bulletin board.

In order to be an outstanding teacher you need to hone your skills through practice, experimentation and more practice. Quietly refining discipline techniques with systematic diligence is a clever way to improve teaching results.

Keeping your Students on Task

Are you having trouble keeping some students on task? Shorten lesson times and make the lesson a little more difficult or easier depending on the particular student who is exhibiting off task behavior.

Compliments

A good ratio of compliments to reprimands is four to one. Give your students four compliments for every reprimand. Do you have a comprehensive reward system in your classroom that your students respond well to collectively and individually? If you do, try challenging yourself with this idea. Go a half or whole school day with compliments only for your students. No reprimands whatsoever!

Contacting Parents

Early in the school year initiate a habit of calling your students' parents regularly. Select an evening a week, perhaps a Friday when you can make about seven calls. This will cover the average size class in about a month. Ongoing contact with parents helps to keep them informed as to their child's progress and may serve to reduce future behavioral problems.

Smile! Smile! Smile!

There is nothing better than a smile, a specific compliment and a large dose of humor on the part of the teacher throughout the day to improve the positive atmosphere between you and your students.

6

Stop Unproductive Behavior Early

Stop unproductive behavior early before it hinders your teaching and students' learning. Misbehavior must be stopped in time, before the situation is totally out of hand. End the misbehavior without rewarding the rule breaker with undue attention and disturbance.

7

Good Organization

Good organization is roughly 80% of good discipline. Have your lessons well planned. Don't allow any down time when students have nothing to do. Have extra activities available at all times.

8

Consistency

The most important aspect in maintaining classroom discipline is consistency. If students are punished for certain offences at some times and not at others, discipline will fall apart. It must be perceived by the students that each individual student is treated with exactly the same consideration, or dissatisfaction will permeate the classroom. Students may lose respect for you and the classroom rules. Students need to know the classroom rules; that the rules will be enforced, and that there are consequences for breaking them.

Don't Make Impossible Demands

Make your demands reasonable. Be sure the students are capable of delivering what you require. Take into consideration such things as age, ability, and the student's emotional state. Be aware of and consider individual differences in intelligence, interests, attitudes and student learning styles.

Your Attitude as a Teacher

Your attitude as a teacher has much to do with how effective you are. You have to develop a positive "mind set." You must not tolerate behavior that disrupts your teaching and any child's learning in your classroom. (See #8 – Consistency)

Start with Specific Praise

Try to ignore the student's misbehavior if it's a minor disturbance. Compliment a student sitting near him for his good behavior or work habits. Be specific. If the student continues to misbehave, then take the next step in your discipline plan for your classroom.

Have an Unobstructed View of Your Class

Don't allow your view of the class to be obstructed when you are checking or correcting students work at your desk or elsewhere in your classroom. Have no more than three students at your correcting station at any one time if you are spending a short time with each student. If you are going into some detail about his work and need a fair amount of time in order to help him then don't have anyone in line. Problem behaviors may develop with students having too much idle time waiting in line.

"I'm Bored"

When a student says "I'm bored" too often, then maybe it's time he was put on an individualized program that matches his ability to the task, with an element of challenge thrown in. If you don't deal with this motivation problem you could be heading for discipline problems with this student. Check the potential for this type of problem early in the school year for every student.

Reasonable Punishment

Pragmatically speaking, punishment does deter children from unacceptable acts. It is your duty to train students to maintain self-control and self-discipline in regards to the rest of society and the world. In later life, many difficult situations will arise. If a state of self-discipline has not been attained, individuals will not be able to cope with many of life's problems. Reasonable punishment with these intentions as an objective is justified.

Be in Control of Yourself

Teaching can be an enjoyable profession. First, you must be in control of your emotions and then in control of your students. Be aware of your emotional state. At the first sign of losing control of yourself in any situation stop what you are doing and do some self-talk. Talk yourself into a more relaxed state of mind and think of a better way to handle the situation. If possible, leave the situation for now and deal with it at some later time. Stabilize the situation first for now.

Don't Use "Try To"

Don't say to a student you want him to try to behave himself or finish his assignments. Trying isn't good enough. It gives him an out. He can say that he tried just like you asked him to. Tell him to do it, not just try to. Don't give him an out!

Create a Reputation Outside Your Classroom

To help you establish a pleasant classroom with a learning atmosphere, cultivate the right reputation outside your classroom.

Before students even meet a particular teacher personally for the first time, they "know" that teacher, or at least they think they do. Part of your task should be to create a "reputation" or image outside the classroom. As a teacher, you are always in contact with students outside the classroom: on the stairways and in the hallways. Your way of interacting in these settings will tell students what kind of a person you are, and what they can expect of you.

Be an "UP" Person

Always give the appearance of being sure of yourself. Look as though you're aware of everything around you. Notice faces when you walk the halls, even if you are in a rush. Look about you and not at the floor. Have that energetic look about you. Have good posture. Show those around you that you are glad to be in the school. Keep your bad days to yourself. Be an "up" person!

(2)

CONTROLLING
LOUDNESS

Controlling Loudness

Quiet Beginnings to a Lesson

The old look at your watch routine works well! If at the beginning of a lesson or after a recess the class is noisy and won't settle down, stand at the front of the room and wait. If you have to wait too long, look at your watch and count the wasted time. When they calm down, stop counting and put the time you waited for them to be quiet on the chalk board and circle it. The class can make up the lost time during the next recess or after school. Often, five or ten seconds of just looking at your watch will quieten them down.

Class Noisy?

If the class is noisy, turn the lights out and count 3, 2, 1, 0 and if they're not quiet, start counting the seconds and threaten to have the class make up the lost time at recess or after school.

The Talkative Student

For the talkative student, inform him that he has an opportunity to be quiet now or at recess. That's his choice. If he chooses to continue to talk, his time is doubled and made up at recess.

When a Group of Students Act Up

When three or four students are acting out at once, the first step in solving this problem is to pick out the one student in the group who is being the most obnoxious. This is not always clear as to who is the most obnoxious. It could cause resentment if you pick the wrong student. Be sure you catch the most obnoxious student if you use this technique. It must be obvious. Stop the misbehavior with this student first. Make eye contact. State the rule he is breaking and the consequence for breaking it. Then go to the second most obnoxious behaving student and so on.

Whole Group Solution to Acting Up

You can deal with a talkative group as a whole. Walk over to the group and make eye contact one by one. Have one of them state the rule broken and the consequence for breaking the rule in question. Alternately state the rule and consequence yourself. This method of dealing with a noisy group is much more productive than yelling at the whole class. If this doesn't work, have a class meeting to discuss ways of solving these types of problems. Student input into solving classroom problems is essential. They are the stakeholders as much as the teacher.

Teaching Whispering

At times it is advantages to allow students the freedom of talking quietly among themselves. A relaxed easy working climate stimulates learning, but children also need a stable controlled environment.

Students need to practice whispering so that they can learn to modulate their voices. Have three or four short lessons of five minutes each over a period of a week or two. Repeat as necessary through the year. Sometimes the students get loud without even realizing it. Have students mingle and whisper to each other. Make it a game, with those not whispering going to one side of the room and standing quietly. You could award prizes or points at this time to those whispering properly.

3

LEAVING THE CLASSROOM

Leaving the Classroom

One at a Time

Allow only one boy and/or one girl to go to the washroom etc. at a time. This reduces any possible behavior or loitering problems. Some students plan to meet their friend out in the hallway or in the washroom at a prearranged time. Watch for this abuse of washroom privileges.

If a Student Asks to Go to the Washroom

Many parents object to their son or daughter not being allowed to go to the washroom on demand. If a student claims he needs to go to the washroom but is often a behavior problem in the hallway or in the washroom, send a trustworthy student with him who is not a best friend of the student who "has to go." Have the trustworthy student report back to you upon their return as to the behavior of the student who claims to need to go to the bathroom. Contact the parents if there's a problem.

Loitering in the Hallway

Here is a possible consequence for students loitering in the hallway or who are late for class. Be sure the students are aware of the consequence ahead of time. If two or three students are being a problem by loitering in the hallway or are late for class on a regular basis, divide the playground up and have them play in separate areas for a while. Prohibit them from being together in the halls and class-room as much as possible.

Class Leaves the Room Noisy

If students are noisy when dismissed, have them sit down again. Say, "Let's try that again." Do this as many times as necessary. They'll get the hang of it once they start feeling like old yoyos.

You Have to Leave the Classroom

If you have to leave the classroom to answer the phone or for whatever reason, assign three monitors to work inde-pendently of each other to write down the names of those who break the rules while you are out. The monitors are not to show the names to any other student or discuss anything with the students while on the job. Collect the three slips of paper from the monitors. If the name of a student is on all three lists, then discipline him by whatever means you feel will teach him the lesson that he must behave himself when you are out of the classroom. Students should not be out of their desks for any reason while you are out of the classroom. Monitors do not answer students' questions. Safety first – back it up. Be firm.

4

POSITIVE / NEGATIVE
CONSEQUENCES

Positive / Negative Consequences

Praise! Praise! Praise!

There can never be too much of the right kind of specific praise directed toward a task and not the person. For example, "Jim, the sentence structure in your paragraph is excellent."

31

Greatest Group Award

Divide the class into four or five groups, depending on the number of students you have and the size of group you would want. Give each group a name or number. Write these names or numbers across the chalk board forming short columns down. Award points to the best group(s) or row(s) who settle down quickly after coming in at recess without wasting time, etc. This can also be helpful to encourage proper behavior when walking to the library or gymnasium. You could give three points to the best group or groups so as not to cause a foot race. Award points at various times of the day. Surprise your students!

The group with the most points at the end of the day becomes the "**Greatest Group**" for the next day. This group has earned the privileges agreed upon by the students such as: first out at recess, first to hand out materials, and so on. Start fresh each day.

Be sure students with behavior problems are evenly distributed among the groups. Groups may give up if they see they have little chance of winning. If you have a student who exhibits severe behavior problems be sure to give every group a turn having him.

Consequences for Breaking Classroom Rules

Consequences depend partly on who breaks the rule in question. A student who has caused problems in the recent past should not be treated lightly. Repeat offenders need to be dealt with more severely. However, you need to give the appearance that you are disciplining the students with equal fairness. The student needs to know the consequences of breaking each rule ahead of time.

The following is just an example of classroom rules. Use it or change it to suit your situation.

Post the Following Under Classroom Rules

Don't overuse this plan as it may cause resentment. Have a sense of how these rules are being accepted by the students. Discuss possible rule changes with the students, if resentment begins to develop.

A very effective means of reducing resentment is to tell the student whose name has been placed on the board that you just want to talk to him for a few minutes about his behavior in class. Tell him that his name is placed on the board as a reminder that the talk will take place.

Warning – name goes on the chalk board

One Check Mark beside the name = 2 minutes detention at recess. His friends leave and he stays behind. It's just enough to inconvenience the student.

Two Check Marks beside the name = 4 minutes detention plus a time out. (Set up a corner of the classroom with a divider so that the student can see you.) Time out away from other class members gives a student a chance to think about what got him into trouble and how to avoid it in the future. Discuss this with him. It also serves as a cooling off period.

Three Check Marks beside the name = same as two check marks plus a loss of privilege: i.e. next earned free time.

Four Check Marks beside the name = 6 minutes detention and time out with four periods of isolation (in class suspension). The student would work on the same lessons as the rest of the class as much as possible without him being in contact with other students.

Five Check Marks beside the name = 15 minutes detention and time out with four periods of isolation.

Six Check Marks beside the name = consult the principal. This could result in an "in school" suspension. Parents should be made aware of these special measures. Parents should be made aware of problems their child is having so that preventive measures can be taken before it gets to this stage. Tell the student you care about him and his education. Therefore, he can't continue to sit with the class for the next day or two or longer. He must know exactly why he is suspended. Use the detention corner or find a special room where he will not be disturbed or disrupt others. Get work for him in line with what the class would be doing. The student loses most of his privileges. Supervise and limit his bathroom breaks (at recess) or any other times he is out of the special area.

Free Periods

Give free periods (in the gym when possible), for those who have not earned a detention as a consequence of breaking the rules. Once per week is fine and on your heaviest teaching day to give you a break. It's a great motivator for many of the students! Find a safe place for the one or two students who haven't earned the free period to work quietly.

The Money Game

The money game is a great positive motivator! This proven game is well liked by students and encourages them to be on task.

The teacher hands out one dollar play money notes to students who are on task, for showing cooperative behavior or for any other ways that students may earn the money. The teacher could walk around the classroom and reward students who are on task. Or, have students come up to your desk to have their assignment spot checked and reward them if they're doing their best work. The teacher could also hand out money to students who enter the classroom quickly and quietly, sit down in their chairs and are ready to begin the next lesson.

Be careful not to hand out too much money during an average school day. See the back of the manual for an example of homemade money. Two or three dollars a day should be about right. Control over the amount of money in circulation in the classroom is important. Too much money handed out could result in too many products or privileges earned. This could cost you a lot of money or you could find it disruptive if too many students have earned privileges at the same time.

This game is a great teaching tool! You could use this game to teach the students how the real world of money supply works; the law of supply and demand. The game can also teach students about choices. They spend their hard earned money. They could invest their money in the "I Can Bank". For example, a student could invest ten dollars and earn one dollar interest per week. Investing could be carried out in lots of ten dollars to simplify things. Have a reliable student monitor run this investment club. The possibilities are endless!

The Money Game Rules

Earn $1.00 for:
- good (productive on-task) behavior
- work well done
- respecting others
- having a positive "I can" attitude

Spend it on:
- $2.00 pencil
- $5.00 pen
- $4.00 scribbler
- $1.00 washroom/drink break
- $10.00 in class free period
- $10.00 in a group of choice for a week
- $10.00 move desk to group or row of choice for a week

Discuss with your students the possible things they can buy. The final choices are yours as you are going to have to come up with these prizes. Select times during the day when you have the time to allow students to spend their money. Allow earned free periods towards the end of the school day. Adjust the rules as you see necessary to suit your classroom situation. Have a student monitor help you hand out money if you like.

More Rules

1. Students can't combine their money with another student's to buy things or go in a group with their friends. In other words lending or borrowing money from other students is not allowed.

2. Any student caught taking or tampering with other student's money will be fined triple that amount. The teacher collects the fine and puts the money back

into the bank to be recirculated to the students who
earn money.

Be careful though to keep this game positive and fun!

Positive Peer Pressure

Put the two or three students who constantly misbehave in
class into a group. For every period these students follow
the classroom rules the class will earn three points (if there
are three students and one point per student). When they
have accumulated ten points the whole class will receive 15
minutes of free time or another reward of choice at a con-
venient time like near the end of the school day. Having
your class earn free time is a great motivator!

5

KEEPING STUDENTS ON TASK

Keeping Students on Task

Student Responsibility

Students must be made to realize that there are both positive and negative consequences that go along with the choices they make. If students do not complete any assignment in class or at home, and they don't know the consequences of their actions, they are really not making a choice or they are making a choice based on insufficient knowledge about the consequences of their actions. The goal is to help students realize that they are responsible for and in control of themselves.

Start Your Class With This Routine

Have a routine your students can follow when they enter your classroom. Think of what you could come up with as a ritual procedure for students to do: perhaps beginning a problem or task you have on the board. This increases the chances of a reasonable start of the period. Students begin by submitting to the structure of the class.

39

Staring

Often, just staring at the disruptive student will make him feel uncomfortable enough to settle down. Stand beside the chalk board where you usually write down the names of students who break the rules. Hold the chalk in your hand for him to see that you are considering placing his name on the chalk board. He should get the message!

40

Sending a Student to the Hall for Misbehavior

If you send a student out into the hall for misbehavior, pin him down (not physically of course). After giving him a minute or so out there, go and talk to him. Tell him that in order for him to get back into the classroom he has to be prepared to do some specific things. Ask him what does "behave yourself" mean? Get a detailed response from him. Have him repeat his response once you are satisfied with it being the right one. Then ask him what is he going to do in order to get back into the classroom? How is he going to behave? Elicit specific answers from him. Don't lecture him. He's probably heard it all before. You have a class to teach so be short. If he can't think of anything, leave him out there for a while longer, then come out and ask him again. If still no proper response comes, leave him out there or send him to the detention area and deal with him later when you have time and perhaps when he is more cooperative.

Set a Goal for Work Expected

Here is a good idea for students who have trouble staying on task. Set a goal for each period for work expected to be completed. Consider the student's ability level. If the student doesn't reach the goal, keep him at recess or after school to finish his work. Tell him it's not a punishment, but that he just needs more time to finish his work and that he's worth the time. This may reduce his anger at being kept in. Phone the parents first to tell them that their little Johnny will be late home if you do keep him after school.

Children Playing with Rulers

Give a warning and/or quietly walk over to the offending student and take the object of this distraction away from him for a while. You may be able to continue teaching as you go about doing this.

Word Study Assignment

A student not on task may be given a word study assignment. Have him look up the following words or make up your own list. He looks up each word in the dictionary and writes down the word and its meaning. He must understand the meanings. Use words such as: cooperation, respect, self-control, confidence, responsible, reliable, and considerate. Explain to him that you may ask him the meaning of the words after and that he had better know them.

Keeping Students Alert

Keeping your students alert and on task can be quite a challenge. When teaching at the front of the whole class or a small group, ask a question first to the whole class or group. Then select a student to answer it. It's great for improving listening skills. If the student can't answer the question because he was not on task tell him to listen carefully, for you may ask him again.

Fun Part Last in a Lesson

Structure your lessons so as to have the fun part after the work has been completed and checked. The work often won't get done if the fun comes first before the work. This greatly reduces possible discipline problems.

In School Suspension

If a student is severely disruptive, and your school has set up a suspension room supervised by staff members, send him there. A suspension room timetable could be set up as it is best if suspended student(s) are always under supervision. Students should be given quiet work. If the student disrupts in the isolation area, add time to his stay. No recess is allowed and lunch is to be eaten in the isolation area. He is escorted to the bathroom. Limit these breaks. He can earn his way back to his classroom by good behavior.

Use Praise to Get Cooperation

When a student is not on task, praise another student who is sitting nearby who is on task. When the offending student gets back on task, be sure to throw a compliment his way. This often works to get a student back on task with little fuss.

A Great Motivator!

Kids often like to get out of work. Use scissors to cut work sheets in half or a green pen to circle sections of the work sheet to be completed. Seeing that they don't have to do the whole sheet motivates them!

Students Finished Work Early

If a student says that he is finished his work, tell him to

think of three sensible things he could do (read, finish a project, math puzzles). Then have him pick one of them and do it. Have him tell you which it is before he starts it.

These "sensible things" could be worked out and agreed to by the teacher and class as an aspect of a classroom meeting.

"Spot Check"

Check at least one sample of student's work completed during any particular part of the day. It keeps them on their toes and lets them know how they're progressing. This is an important aspect of your evaluation process. If you find that a large number of students are having the same problem in math for example, have some or all of your students hand in all of their assignment for a "spot check" after every lesson. You'll catch the laggards and help create good work habits. This will keep you busy but it will tend to keep your students on task. This idea catches problems early, perhaps after a student completes two incorrect answers rather than ten.

Name on Chalk Board Gets Results

Here is a great old idea! Tell a student that you will write his name on the board or on a piece of paper for being disruptive and you will see him later about his unproductive behavior. He will often shape up with this little idea. He may be afraid of "wasting my recess" talking to the teacher.

Red Light Green Light Controls Behavior

When you want your class to behave in a certain manner for a specific period then use a traffic light. Cut out red and green circles from construction paper. Hang up the appropriate color at the front of the room.

Red Light = Quiet work time in your desk
Green Light = Whispering is allowed
An orange light could be added for encouraging any other desired behavior.

Timing Tasks

Cut down on the usual time you allow to finish an assignment. Inform your students that you will time them using a timer and that they are expected to work as quickly and as carefully as possible until the buzzer goes off. On-task behavior and higher productivity should result from occasionally timing tasks.

6

IMPROVING
STUDENT - TEACHER
RELATIONSHIPS

Improving Student - Teacher Relationships

Strive To Be Calm At All Times

Use your method of discipline. Plug in whichever technique that suits the occasion. Before reacting to a problem situation, think about how your reaction to it fits in with your overall plan for creating and maintaining a positive classroom environment. Don't get angry and raise your voice, although used sparingly, feigning anger has an amazing effect.

Generally your anger is the least effective motivation. Anger should not be part of a correct formula for controlling children, while maintaining a positive atmosphere in your classroom. Be firm. Be calm.

Listen! Listen! Listen!

It is not wise to lecture and warn. Be ready to listen to the student's side of the story. If you are not ready to listen, then don't ask the student what happened. If you don't listen it will be one-sided as far as students are concerned and they will not respond. Their attitude will not change as their energy will be channelled into their need to defend themselves. So, use eye contact and let the student know

43

that he is the most important person to you in the whole wide world at that moment.

The Most Important Element Is The Relationship

A loving caring relationship between teacher and child is most important. A child needs to know that you have a genuine affection for him. When the opportunity arises, tell him you like him, you care about him, and you're glad he's in your class (even if you don't, it's your professional duty to do so). If he thinks you don't like him, he will act accordingly.

Remedial Help

If there is nothing specific in a student's work deserving honest praise then it's perhaps time to offer remedial help. Select one or two recesses or another time to help him with problem areas.

Approaching Students in the Hallway

Suppose you spot a student you wish to speak with on the other side of the hall. Go a step or two past this student, turn around, walk with the traffic, and then approach the student on the diagonal. When you think about where to stop, consider where the student is standing. If the student is standing in the hall, then stand on the diagonal, facing him. If the student is leaning with his back against the wall, then diagonally move up near him on the wall, lean against the wall, turning slightly sideways towards the student.

From either position, start with a personal greeting. From this position, you will be less threatening, less "in the face" of the student, and that is a form of respect.

The important thing for you to remember is to use every opportunity to treat students respectfully, politely and pleasantly. It takes very little time for the word to get out that you are an OK dude and not a critic always pulling rank.

More Praise

One of the first things to use is praise and specific feedback. Praise by itself is not enough. You need to pay attention to the action and not the act. For example: good writing, proper slant of letters, correct height of letters.

Praise by:
> **Auditory** – "Very good".
> **Visual** – Smile or written praise
> **Physical** – Touch his arm or shoulder.
> *(Be careful with this one).*

Two Children Having A Problem

If two children have a problem, it is often best to just let them work it out by themselves. Let them resolve the conflict. Have them put their hands behind their backs, face each other and talk the problem out. Children don't moralize as teachers do.

Students Bugging Other Students At Recess

If a student is constantly bugging another student, send the hostile student to a corner of the playground. That's his playground for a while. Or, have him walk to the far fence bordering the playground and back, a specific number of times.

7

STUDENT
SELF ASSESSMENT
PROGRAM

Student Self Assessment Program

Self-Assessment Program

The Self-Assessment Program is a technique which can help students assess and modify their own behavior. It is better than handing out lines which is objectionable to some as a waste of time as it teaches little. Have a student copy his sheet at least once. Sit down with the student afterwards if you feel it beneficial and go through the sheet discussing each point.

Enclosed at the back of this manual are examples covering a few areas of concern. You could make up your own to fit any particular problem situation.

⑧

OVERCOMING NEGATIVE ATTITUDES

Overcoming Negative Attitudes

Con Games

Don't be conned (tricked) with con games. "I had my hand up. You didn't help. Don't blame me."

Begging, Bribing

"Please, let me have recess. I promise I'll do it for home-work tonight."

Sulking

"I'm not going to do any work. I'm just going to sit here." By not getting caught up in these con games, you stay in control of yourself thereby promoting a learning environ-ment. You don't get angry and give in to begging. Do not reinforce sulking behavior with offers of help.

Bad Language

Children bring attitude problems into the school. Attitude problems are a reflection of society but we must try to curb unacceptable language and behavior. Remember, the school is not an extension of the street. Don't tolerate obscene language or inappropriate behavior in the school. It must stop when the child crosses the sidewalk into the school grounds. Relate these points to the student.

Vulgar T-Shirt

Here's what you can do about a child who comes to school wearing a vulgar t-shirt. Note the other children's reaction to the wearing of that t-shirt. If the t-shirt distracts the students from their learning then you may have a case for asking the wearer of the offending t-shirt to put on a sweater or jacket over top of it for now until a change of t-shirt can be arranged.

Some parents may be upset if you don't come up with a reason they can live with. Don't focus on the belief that the t-shirt is obscene. Tell the parent that anything that disrupts learning in the school is not allowed. The school is not an extension of the street and that kind of thing must not enter the school grounds in any form.

9

STUDENT
CONTRACTS

Student Contracts

Behavioral Contracts

A Behavioral Contract can work on students with behavioral problems as it is a structured procedure: an agreement between you and the student. For example, if the student fails to complete an assignment in the given time limit he can finish the work after school. Provide the student with an opportunity to earn a positive consequence if the assignment was completed on time.

Behavior Modification Tracking Sheet

The behavior modification tracking sheet is an instrument which can track a student's attitude and behavior throughout the school day. Problem areas or classes can be noted and remedial measures taken. The student carries the sheet on a clipboard around with him. After each class he hands it to the teacher with a pen, to be completed with either a positive or negative comment made about the student's performance during the class. This sheet is very useful for parent-teacher interviews. See the back of the manual for a copy of a contract.

70

Contract

Date _____

_____ will rejoin the class after sus-
pension, one step at a time (see steps below). He will move
down one number at a time spending one day at each step.
If he has had a day where his behavior has not been acceptable, he will go up (back) a number: example: 3 to 4.

Signed

_____

_____

Steps To Returning To Being A Regular Member Of The Class

He will then enjoy all the rights and privileges other class
members have.

#4 Isolation from all students using a room divider, etc.
    He must not see or talk to any other student during
    class time.
#3 Sit behind the teacher facing the front of the class-
    room with his back to the students.
#2 Sit beside the teacher's desk with his back to the
    students.
#1 He has earned his way back to his place with the
    class.

The student in question has the responsibility for moving his desk at the right appropriate time.

Rules:
    a. for one day (eight periods) change as needed
    b. seven or eight periods of 2's or 3's he steps down a number
    c. five or six periods of 2's or 3's he stays where he is
    d. four or fewer periods of 2's or 3's he steps up a number

Strategy For Behavior Change

Conference with a Student

#1   **Establish Rapport**
Let the student know that you like him as a person. He's expecting something else (a loud lecture???)

#2   **Determine the Nature of the Undesirable Behavior**
Talk to others who may be involved. What's happened? Why is he in trouble? Ask him.

#3   **Determine the Causes of the Behavior**
"What led up to the problem situation?"
"What was your part in it?"
Don't accept any excuses.
You are not asking why did you do it but what led up to the problem situation.
Obtain as specific an answer as possible.

#4   **Obtain a Value Judgment from the Student**
"Is it helping you to do this? Is it helping your teacher?

Is it helping others?"

#5   Identify Payoffs
What are the benefits associated with the behavior, the rewards for the student?

#6   Identify Costs
What does it cost the student to behave in that fashion? Example: *"I got kicked out of school."* Determine if the student thinks that the cost is worth it. Maybe he likes doing it.

#7   What Could He Have Done Differently?
Ask the student, "What could you do that would work out better?" Obtain a specific answer from the student: "I will do my Math assignment."

#8   Get a Commitment
Obtain a short term commitment from him. What could he do differently. "I will complete my Math assignment for the next class period." You could arrange a verbal or written plan over time.

#9   Methods
Identify methods for accomplishing the new behavior.

#10   Handshake!
End the session with a handshake and a smile to let him know you like him and care about him.

Checkup

To be sure that a short term commitment has been completed you need to check up on the student as often as specified in that commitment.

Use Positive Reinforcements

The student needs to be positively reinforced as he continues on task. Be as private and specific as possible in the reinforcement. Be sincere.

Extend the Commitment

As involvement occurs, keep extending the time for the student's commitment, to the point where he is functioning independently.

Consequences for no Improvement

If no improvement occurs, build into the plan some consequences. In this strategy, consequences are not or may not be introduced until this step. Specific consequences could include isolation in the detention area or loss of participation in extra activities such as house leagues, lunch, recess or playground games. He still gets lunch!

10

PROBLEM SOLVING TECHNIQUES / MEDIATION

Problem Solving Techniques / Mediation

Cousin Klemm's Secret Formula For Solving Problems When Two People Disagree

This is a great win/win formula that gets the two students listening to each other which results in problems being solved!

Method

#1   Agree
Both parties need to agree that they want to solve the problem.

#2   Listen
"I'll listen to you if you'll listen to me." Listen to the other person's side of the story and paraphrase back that he said for understanding. Reverse the order until the problem situation is talked out and fully understood by both parties.

#3   Solve It
Once you know the problem, try to solve it. With your help have students think of three or four possible solutions and select one to try. It must be agreed on by both parties. If it doesn't solve the problem or at least make the problem bearable then agree to meet again to select another possible solution to try.

Rules

#1   **Don't argue**
#2   **No name calling**
#3   **One person speaks at a time**

Role Play

Role play this technique by selecting a few students (those that are skilled role models) to make up a problem situation and solve it. Post the method on a display board under the heading so students can learn this formula and use it even when you are not around to help them. Turn this problem situation into an opportunity to learn.

Teach Social Skills

Social skills can also be taught during these sessions. You may inquire, "What do you do when you feel angry?" After the response, ask, "What is the best thing to do?" Of course you would need to tailor the meeting to your own particular counselling style and the classroom situation. This method works well to improve cooperation within the classroom.

The Round Table (discussion group)

Here is a great tool for teaching students problem solving and for improving relationship skills. Students become more responsible, more human and pick up some great ideas for dealing with situations involving other children. Basically the method involves whole class discussion of problem situations that arise and may involve other students or even the teacher. Be wary of unprofessional conduct!

Method

#1   Students place their concerns in writing in the Round Table box to go on the agenda for the next meeting. Have each student submitting a concern include their name. Students know that something bothering them will be dealt with.

Often, this action alone serves to give them time to cool down and work out the problem themselves before it comes up at the meeting.

#2   You would then go through the written concerns in the Round Table box. Select the most important ones that will be dealt with first.

#3   Short 10 to 30 minutes could be held a few times per week to go over these concerns. Regularly held sessions help to get past dealing with the surface or presenting problem, permitting opportunities to deal with the real deeper problems.

#4   You may want to have a secretary record (take minutes) the concerns so that you can follow up on the matter at the next session. Ask the students involved, "How did that work out?" In that way, the deeper problem hopefully will be successfully dealt with.

#5   Begin the whole class or group session with compliments. First express praise and encourage students to likewise compliment fellow students. Be sure to include less worthy students in your compliments so that they too can feel a part of this process in a positive way.

Example: "I really appreciate Johnny for sharing his lunch with Mike today." Shy away from giving compliments for material possessions like clothing. Direct compliments to the student's character, behavior or attitude.

#6   Play soft background music such as the sound of birds chirping.

Steps to Problem Solving

#1   The teacher or a student would then explain the problem in easy understandable language.

#2   Discuss the problem pointing out that discussions are to be carried out with respect in mind for fellow classmates. No name calling or blaming are allowed.

#3   Ask for solutions from the students; at first from the students directly involved in the problem situation and then from the others. If no solutions are forth coming then you can suggest a number of them. The students can usually come up with some as they don't like to get them from you.

An example of the presenting problem not being the real problem is the water fountain fight. Students tussle to be the first to have a drink. This seems to be a straightforward problem, but on further investigation the cause was that students wanted to be the first in class so they could sit by you. A schedule where students take their turn might solve that problem.

#4 It is a good idea to occasionally review the steps with the students by going over a problem just recently worked on. This reinforces the skills of the problem solving.

A Persistent Fighter

When a student does not respond to warnings for fighting, take him to the office and phone home. When a parent answers, explain that the child has had another fight. Hand the phone over to him and tell him to tell the parent the whole story. You be next to him as he relates the story. This ensures that the parent gets the straight story. This also gives the parent time to think how to deal with the little scrapper when he gets home.

11

DISRESPECT /
DEFIANCE

Disrespect / Defiance

Rebellious vs. "Challenging" Behavior

Be careful to distinguish "rebellious" behavior distinctly different in origin from "challenging" defiance. A child may feel frustrated, disappointed or rejected. A teacher must move quickly to pacify the cause. Try to understand how the child is feeling. The art of good teaching revolves around the interpretation of meaning behind behavior. The most vital objective of disciplining a child is to gain and maintain his respect. Fail this and you're in for a tough year.

Protect The Socially–Rejected Child

Protect the child that is socially rejected by the others. Respond to rejection in this general theme: "What right do any of you have to be so mean to _____? Which of you is perfect that the rest of us couldn't make fun of you or pick on you? I know you and can easily think of something about you or your home that we can laugh at. I could make you feel really bad. But I won't. I would never embarrass you in any way because it hurts to be laughed at by the people you know. That doesn't mean that the person you're picking on is without fault. All of you are equally important to me. But if you pick on _____, then I'm on his/her side. You'll be picking on me and I don't like being picked on."

When A Request Gets A "No"

When you ask a student to come up to you at your desk, he may say "no." If he does then repeat the request. If he still says "no", then tell him to stay there. Get your attention onto something else before he says "no" again. This bail out technique allows you to win both ways. He stays or he comes up. Tell him you will speak to him later about the matter. The class is not disrupted this way. He doesn't win the eyes of the other students and you save face.

You'll Lose If You Argue!

Refuse to argue with anyone who understands English as you will most likely lose. There are more questions than answers and children seldom run out of questions to ask. Say: "I understand what you're saying but the point is ...." Don't get sidetracked.

12

SETTING
DOWN
THE RULES

Setting Down the Rules

Teacher Punctuality

It is important that a good example be set to the students in regards to punctuality. You should be on the job at times required by the school act and demonstrate to the students the importance of being punctual.

Student Punctuality

If a student is late on a regular basis, keep track of the number of minutes late and have the student serve double that time at recess or after school. Discuss the issue with the student and perhaps the parents, to help with getting the student back on schedule.

There may be a good reason for his being late. Speak with him. For example, he may be arriving at school at 9:05 A.M. because his parents don't want him beaten up or picked on when he goes to school.

Forgetting School Materials

Students forgetting their school materials (pens, pencils, etc.) need to be dealt with because it is disruptive and time wasting. Announce to the students that you have extra pens, pencils and books which they could borrow. If they forget to bring their materials, all they have to do is ask for a loan. There is one hitch. The borrowing student would have to stand for a predetermined length of time depending on the age level and the particular student. He could stand by a desk at the back of the room. If any written work is required, he has to lean over his desk from a standing position. Limit this idea to one or two students at a time, otherwise it could be disruptive.

Identify the Rules

Identify the rules well in advance. Let there be no doubt about what is and is not acceptable behavior. Direct challenges to your authority as a teacher in the case of willful, haughty disobedience requires strong action. When a child expresses a defiant "No," you had better take it out of him. It is a question of who is in charge here and if you're not firm and answer the question conclusively for the child, then he will battle you over and over. Children want to know their boundaries but they want you to earn the right to control them. However, discipline and loving kindness are not opposites; one is a function of the other. *Criticize the act and not the person.*

Don't Accept Excuses

Refuse to accept excuses. Proper rules lead to consequences for inappropriate behavior. However, listen to reasons.

Group Students With Severe Discipline Problems

If you have one, two or three students who don't respond well to the regular classroom rules and continue to misbehave and disrupt the class then put them into a separate group of their own and have the positive consequences the same as the rest of the students but have negative consequences much more severe. In a short period of time this should improve their behavior well enough to return to the regular classroom rules.

Have A Wide Range Of Consequences

For rule violations it is a good idea to have at least two consequences to draw on for each type of violation. This gives you flexibility to meet specific needs while still being consistent. Be sure to explain your reasons in advance for having different consequences.

Lunchroom Rules

#1 Stay in your own desk
#2 Speak softly
#3 Eat your food, don't throw it
#4 Keep your eating area clean
#5 Ask permission from the lunch supervisor before going for a drink of water or to go to the washroom.

Consequences For Not Following The Lunchroom Rules

#1 Eat by yourself away from your classmates.
#2 Suspension from lunchroom, student eats elsewhere in the school by himself.
#3 The student will eat his lunch at home or he has to have his parent's signature handed into lunchroom supervisor before being allowed to return.

Get Close To A Student When Disciplining

It is far more effective if you are close to a student when explaining a rule or consequence. Calmly walk over to the student at a conversation distance, about an arm's length away for junior or senior high school students and then a step closer. With younger students you can move even closer. Make direct eye contact if possible as you deliver the rule and consequence. Be aware that in some cultures it is a sign of disrespect to have eye contact or to invade someone's personal space.

Classroom Rules

Rules are most important to all discipline programs. Rules that are vague give students difficulty in making the connection between their behavior and the consequences of any productive or unproductive behavior.

I have deliberately kept the rules short and to the point. Use of these rules of discipline or any other depends on the method of teaching you favour and often at what stage in the lesson you are teaching. Be flexible – don't be afraid to alter a rule for a particular segment of a lesson or for a whole lesson depending on whether you want any student to respond to a question or if you want certain students to respond so as to ascertain whether a concept taught has been learned.

Post the rules and consequences in the classroom for the students and other teachers to see and be aware of. Have as many or as few rules as you deem important. The fewer the better though. Have students participate in formulating acceptable and desirable behaviors as well as consequences for not following **their** rules.

90

Rules

#1 Follow directions
#2 Be quiet – and listen when the teacher is talking
#3 Keep objects to yourself (pens, pencils, etc).
      SAFETY FIRST.
#4 Respect the rights of your teacher and fellow students
      so that your rights will also be respected

91

Positive Consequences

#1 Free time
#2 First in line
#3 Reward coupons
#4 Hand out monitor
#5 Treats
#6 Sit by a friend for a day
#7 Other good things

92

Negative Consequences

#1 Warning
#2 Loss recess time

#3   Penalty box – placed in a corner away from other students

#4   Time out in the hallway, detention room and a phone call home.
IT'S YOUR CHOICE!!!

Penalty Box

The penalty box is a quiet corner of the classroom where a student can be away from the other students because of being uncooperative.

Rules

#1   Sit quietly

#2   Be ready and do your work

#3   Permission needed to leave your desk.

Consequences – if rule broken

#1   Write out choice helper (see back of manual for copy) and discuss it with your teacher. Take the choice helper home and have a parent sign it. If not signed and returned: parent phoned.

#2   If you are not cooperating you will leave the room and sit in a desk in the hallway or detention room. Your parent will be phoned and asked to come in for a conference.

13

REDUCING
STRESS

Reducing Stress

Use Audio Visual Aids

Have a supply of audio visual aids on hand such as film strips, videos, or films for use when you need a break from the constant contact with your students. Bring in guest speakers such as parents or local resource people to speak on subjects of interest to the students. Combine classes with another teacher and share the break. These ideas put to use can give you the quiet time you need that will help you manage stress and avoid burnout.

Reduce Extra-Curricular Activities

It is very easy to get overextended with extra-curricular activities that can sap your energy and leave you with little enthusiasm for your teaching responsibilities. Cut down where possible and plan ahead so as not to get overextended again in the future.

On the other hand, doing some extra-curricular activities rather than none lets you and your students see each other perform in a less formalized setting. This is usually a positive step in relating to students.

Correcting Students' Work

Limit your correcting of students' work to all you can correct in one hour a day. Assign work accordingly.

Yelling Doesn't Work!

Yelling at your students for an extended period of time will drain you of your energy. Loud talking also raises blood pressure. You must find other means of getting your students cooperation. There are many ideas in this manual that will help you out.

Enjoy Your Evenings

Spend two or three evenings a week doing the things you enjoy. Get away from your job and thoughts of it. Indulge yourself in a pleasurable hobby.

Take Ten Minutes To Relax

Find ten minutes during the school day and go to a quiet place and relax. Get a small tape player and listen to a relaxation tape or just think relaxing thoughts. Do this at least once a day and you will be greatly refreshed.

Responding To Problems Emotionally Saps Energy

Wait a few seconds before responding to a problem situation. This reduces tension and helps you to respond in a non-emotional way. This can teach the students to do likewise.

A Stress-Reducing Breathing Technique

When you find yourself in a stressful situation deep breathing is sure to help. You can virtually counteract your body's stress response by concentrating on breathing slowly and deeply for a time.

Take a Lunch-Hour Walk

There is nothing like a stress-busting lunch-hour walk to get your mind off distressing concerns and give you a feeling of detachment from the day's aggravations. By relaxing and freeing your thoughts to wander you may be able to see a stressful situation in a new light. And who knows, you may even find a solution to the problem.

14

WHOLE SCHOOL TECHNIQUES

Whole School Techniques

Frank Sinatra Club

Here's a technique that will encourage students not to earn their way back into the suspension room and it's lots of fun! Secure one of Frank Sinatra's music tapes and play it while the suspension room is occupied with a student or students. Frankie will make their stay a rather unpleasant one. Some may even grow to like his rather uncool music. Make up a poster to place on a bulletin board for the students to see. Your poster might include these words. Hi! My name is <u>Frank Sinatra</u>. I hope you enjoy my singing! If you don't, then next time <u>make a more responsible choice</u>. <u>Right choice</u> = (you can draw a happy face on the poster next to right choice). <u>Wrong choice</u> – more of Frankie's favorites. <u>It's your choice</u>!!!

Make an extra copy or two as these tapes have been known to disappear. Tape the original onto a ninety minute tape so that you don't have to turn the tape over so often. For a change of pace try a tape of Wilf Carter, Stomping Tom Connors, or Tiny Tim!

Outside Recess Detention

Select an area in the playground against the school where students can be placed to serve a recess suspension. Students must stay within the boundaries of this area. Adults on supervision need to be made aware of any student placed in suspension in this fashion. Other students may not step within this area. Detention could be for any length of time deemed necessary. Students could be told that their time in suspension could be reduced with good behavior. Place a clipboard on the wall just inside the outside door with the student's name on a sheet, so that teachers on duty are aware of who is on "the sheet".

Green Slips For Documentation

A green slip is used to report a discipline problem that has occurred. A green slip can be used to report misbehavior in the hallways, in the playground or in a classroom. Teachers coming in to teach in a classroom that is not their homeroom can use green slips to report students involved in off-task behavior. There are a number of ways this technique can be put to use. However, do not overuse it as this will tend to water down its effectiveness. Have a large number of green slips made up and stapled together in packets of ten or so. Place green slip holders on bulletin boards in the hallways around the school.

Teachers who fill out the green slips should return them to the student's homeroom teacher. The teacher will place the slip into a scribbler which has the pages marked off alphabetically. The slip would go under the letter which begins the student's last name. This technique provides the teacher with documentation which would be helpful during the next parent-teacher interview. See the back of the manual for an example of a green slip which can be photocopied and used.

The Penalty Box

The penalty box is a technique which provides a negative consequence for students who are not cooperating for any reason. Students would miss playing and/or watching a specific number of house league games or any other activity in the gymnasium or playground. An alternative to this is for the student to miss activities for a specified length of time. A sheet would be placed on the bulletin board just outside the gymnasium with a small envelope containing a few pencils. Written on this sheet is the student's name, the date he went into the penalty box and the date he leaves. The teacher supervising the activity would be informed of the student's exclusion from the activity and he would make sure the student is not watching or is engaged in the activity.

107

Reading Settles Students Down

Students can learn to settle down quickly after coming into class by using this idea. Immediately upon the students entering the classroom and returning to their desks or work stations, they are to take out a book to read for five minutes. Use this idea every time the students come into class. Establish the idea as a routine. This gives the teacher time to settle in after perhaps a recess duty and get prepared for the next lessons to teach. This idea could be used by all classrooms in a wing of the school as an aid to clearing the hallways.

108

Violence-Free Zone Posters

Violence-Free Zone posters can be placed around the school to remind students that the school is a violence-free zone where no violence of any kind will be permitted. The students are given an expectation to live up to. This concept could be introduced and explained to the student body during an assembly, preferably early in the school year. See the back of the manual for a sample of a poster that you can reproduce.

Keeping The School Clean Award

The "Golden Garbage Can Award" is presented weekly to all the students of the classroom that shows the most responsibility and team spirit in keeping their classroom, their locker area, (if there is one) and the rest of the school clean and tidy. The award consists of a metal garbage can painted gold and perhaps a trophy to sit on top of the upside down can. Also, a certificate is awarded which the class can hang up and brag about.

Student Crime Stoppers

Here's a program that is making quite a difference to a Toronto-area high school. The secondary school has experienced a dramatic reduction in crime since instituting the Student Crime Stoppers program.

Students are asked to take charge of their own school environment and do something about the people who are threatening students, stealing things, and damaging property.

A staff liaison person like a guidance counselor is needed to set up and run the program. Also needed is a five-member student board.

The program is designed to identify unacceptable behavior at an early stage and correct it.

A variety of punishments can be used, from suspension to community service.

For more details contact Crime Stoppers.

This program may not be available in your area. Another organization may offer a similar program.

When A New Student Violates A Rule

When a new student violates a school or classroom rule, simply saying "I know you are new here, but we don't behave that way at this school" may result in future conformity. To help both new and returning students avoid problems, prepare a Student Guide with input from students and parents.

Written at the students' level of understanding, the Guide will explain both the school's culture as well as established discipline procedures to students and their parents. Assigning students in each homeroom to mentor new students can also assist them in getting off to a good start.

Attitude is Everything

The longer I live the more I realize the impact of attitude on my life. Attitude to me is more important than anything else in life. Whatever results we get from life is determined for the most part by our attitude. Our attitude determines the attitude of others toward us. The actions, feelings, or thoughts of others toward us will be determined by our actions, feelings, or thoughts toward them. This in turn controls to a large degree our success or failure in any endeavour. It is then, our attitude toward life which will determine life's attitude toward us.

Everything operates on the law of cause and effect. Good attitude: good results. Average attitude: average results. Bad attitude: bad results. We shape our own life and the shape of it is determined by our own attitude. Our attitude is a reflection of what is happening on the inside. The remarkable thing is we have a choice every day regarding the attitude we will embrace for that day. We cannot change our past, or other people. The one thing we can do is to play on the one string we have: and that is our attitude.

How does a person make this kind of good attitude a habit? It's most easily done by first conducting yourself as though you already have a positive expectant attitude toward life. You must become mentally from an attitude standpoint, the person you want to be.

How do we do this? Well, we want certain results from the world based on our actions, feelings, or thoughts. To bring about those results we must act toward the world with an attitude calculated to produce the results we want. For example, if we want others to treat us with respect and admiration then we must treat others with respect and admiration first. Treat every person as the most important person on earth.

You'll notice how quickly it develops into a habit. Almost immediately you will notice a change. Irritations that use to frustrate and trouble you will vanish. When some person gives you a difficult time, stay on course. Don't let another person control your attitude. Don't let another person's unhappiness make you unhappy. Don't waste time talking about your problems or your poor health unless you're talking to your doctor. Radiate the attitude of success and confidence.

Treat everyone with whom you come in contact with, without exception, as the most important person on earth. Start this habit. Practice it constantly and you'll do it the rest of your life. I am convinced that life is 10% what happens to me and 90% how I react to it.

Choice Helper

Name: _____ Grade: _____ Date: _____

What Happened:

_____
_____
_____
_____

What Choice I Made That Caused The Problem:

_____
_____
_____
_____

What Better Choice(s) Could I Have Made:

_____
_____
_____
_____

Teacher's Comments:

_____
_____
_____
_____

Teacher _____

Principal's Comments:

_____
_____
_____

Principal _____

Parent's Signature _____

Self-Assessment Program

Fighting / Hitting Others

1. **What did I do wrong?** I was fighting / hitting another student

2. **What is wrong with fighting / hitting another student?**
   I might hurt the other student or get hurt myself. I might have other consequences to face because of my actions. We might have to go to the principal about it.

3. **What should I do instead of fighting/hitting?**
   A. Stop and count to ten – especially if I am angry.
   B. Think about my choices:
   1) Walk away for now
   2) Talk to the person in a friendly way.
   3) Ask someone for help in solving the problem: a teacher
   C. Act out my best choice and try another if my first choice doesn't work.

4. **Why should I not fight or hit others?** Fighting is only one way to resolve matters and there are other grown-up ways too. (See number 3. above). Someone might be seriously hurt and have to go to the hospital. That could cause more problems for both families of the students involved. It's better not to fight. Next time I will make a better choice!

_____
Student's Signature

_____
Parent's Signature

_____
Teacher's Signature

Self-Assessment Program

Talking Too Loud

1. **What did I do wrong?** I was talking too loud.

2. **What is wrong with talking too loud?** Talking too loud shows little respect for other students and for my teacher. By talking too loud and not whispering I am forcing others to talk louder to be heard. This causes the noise level in the classroom to be excessive (too loud). Loud noise is irritating and hard on people's ears. If I talk too loud I will have to write an essay like this one or stay in at recess.

3. **What should I have been doing instead of talking too loud?** I should have been whispering at no more than arm's length to the person I wish to talk to. I should move closer to that person so I don't have to shout.

4. **Why should I have been whispering and not talking loudly?** I would show respect for my fellow students, my teacher and their right to work in a reasonably quiet environment (classroom). Loud noise is irritating and gives some people headaches. It also makes us tired. There is a much more pleasant atmosphere in the classroom when everyone whispers and does not shout out loud.

_____
Student's Signature

_____
Parent's Signature

_____
Teacher's Signature

Behavior Modification Tracking Sheet

Date: _____   Student Name: _____

Subject/Class	Attitude/Behavior			Teacher's initial
Math	1	2	3	
Language Arts	1	2	3	
Reading	1	2	3	
Science	1	2	3	
Social	1	2	3	
Music	1	2	3	
Art	1	2	3	
Physical Education	1	2	3	
Other	1	2	3	

Circle one of the above per class
1 - Excellent
2 - Satisfactory
3 - Unsatisfactory
(state why with a comment
if teacher feels it's necessary)

Parent's Signature _____

Green Slips

Discipline Report

Student _____ Homeroom_____ Date _____

Time of Day: (check one) AM____ Noon ____ PM ____

Student Action _____Teacher Action_____
_____
_____
_____

Student signs _____ Teacher signs_____

Discipline Report

Student _____ Homeroom_____ Date _____

Time of Day: (check one) AM____ Noon ____ PM ____

Student Action _____ Teacher Action _____
_____
_____
_____

Student signs _____ Teacher signs _____

Discipline Report

Student _____ Homeroom_____ Date _____

Time of Day: (check one) AM____ Noon ____ PM ____

Student Action _____ Teacher Action _____
_____
_____
_____

Student signs _____ Teacher signs _____

VIOLENCE FREE ZONE

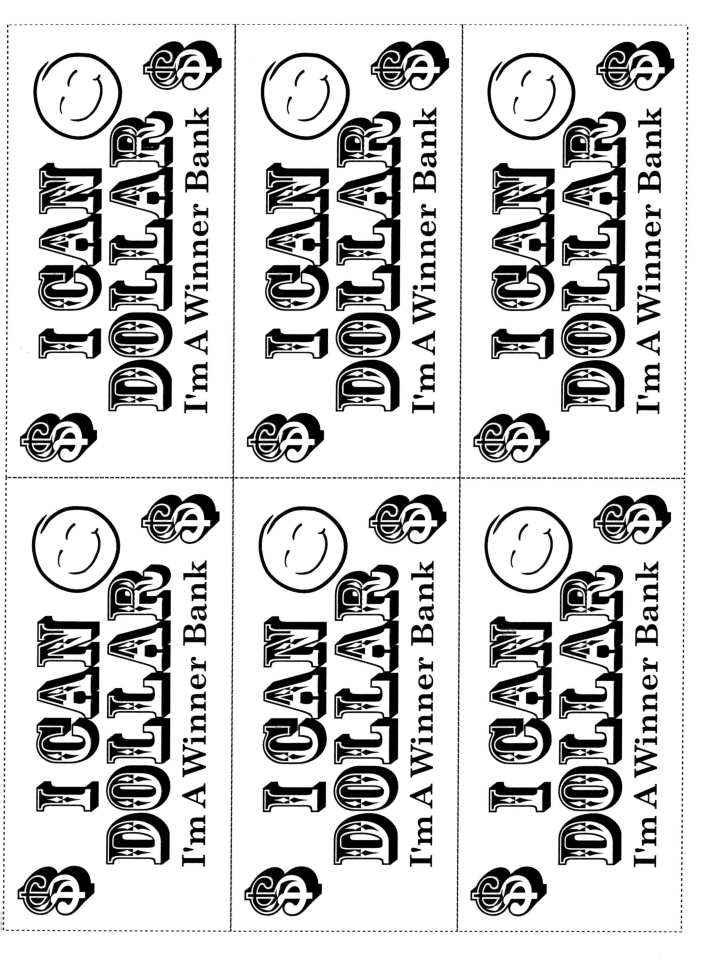

NOTES

NOTES

NOTES

NOTES

NOTES

About the Author

Mervin Hempel is a retired school teacher and guidance counselor who lives with his wife Judy in Victoria on Vancouver Island, on the west coast of Canada. They have two grown children.

Born in eastern Canada, Mervin has travelled extensively and has taught, tutored, and counselled in urban and suburban neighbour-hoods in various schools in Canada and Australia. He was edu-cated at the University of Winnipeg and the University of Manitoba.

He has been 49 years old for the past nine years, because he likes that age. Hiking the coastline around the southern part of the Island, cycling the trails, and walking his dog are three of his favorite outdoor activities. He also reads, writes and spends way too much time on the computer playing chess with his buddies from around the world.

ISBN 141200850-6